That's So Pacific Northwest Coloring Book

25 Whimsical Illustrations to Color and Enjoy

By Heather Douglas

That's So Pacific Northwest Coloring Book

© 2016 Heather Douglas

oscarastoria.com
facebook.com/oscarastoria/

That's So Pacific Northwest Coloring Book

Table of Contents

This book is dedicated to my mom.

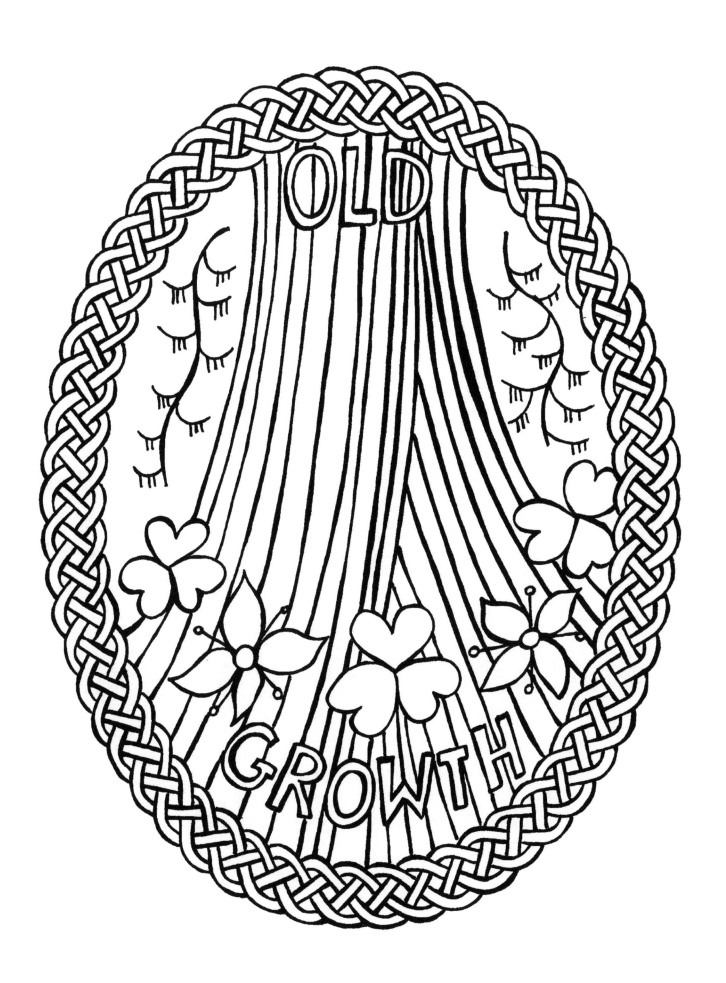

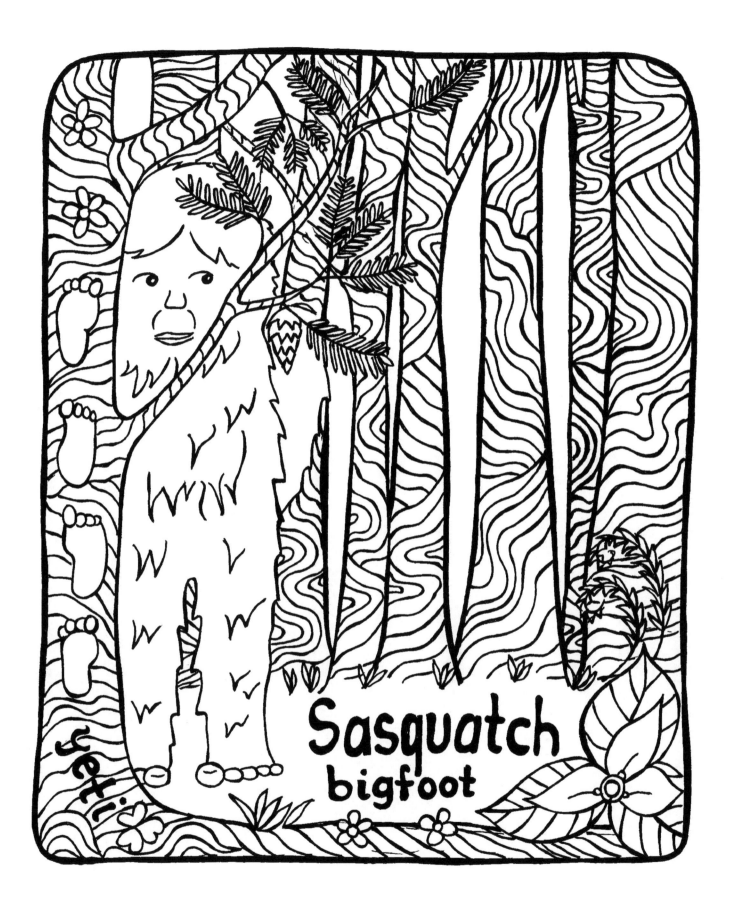

Sasquatch
bigfoot

yeti

Gentle Ben Walt Morey

Turtle Island G. Snyder

owls of the PNW

Ursula K. LeGuin

Diary of a Part-time Indian

hiking

independent ♥ book stores

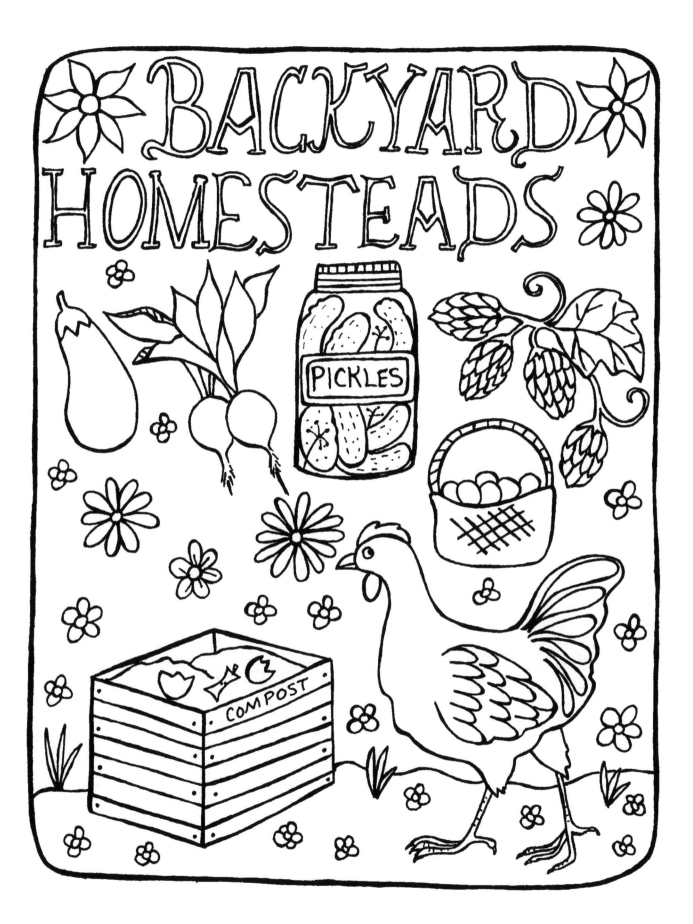

notes

notes

. . . .

About the Illustrator

Heather Douglas is a freelance illustrator, writer and educator. She was born and raised in Astoria, Oregon. For more information about the author, the creation of this book and other projects, visit her website and Facebook page.

Thank you for supporting a local artist!

Contact
Heather Douglas
Oscar Astoria
P.O. Box 1092
Astoria, Oregon 97103

oscarastoria.com
facebook.com/oscarastoria/

Made in the USA
Columbia, SC
30 November 2017